JUST A WALK WITH GOD

JUST A WALK WITH GOD

DEE WASHINGTON

© 2016 Dee Washington
All rights reserved.
ISBN: 098634561X
ISBN-13: 9780986345616
Library of Congress Control Number: 2016933979
Prime Warriors Publishing: Columbus, Ohio

To all mankind:

It is my hope that you will find joy and encouragement from the Lord while reading the poems in this book. Thank you for your support!

CONTENTS

Acknowledgments · ix

Choose Me · 1
Pain So Deep · 2
Who Do You Choose? · 3
You are Somebody · 4
So Tired, My God · 6
The Children Teach You · 7
Flawed: So Why the Judgment? · 8
Love in My Heart · 9
Anger · 10
Love is You · 11
Bondage · 12
Fairy Tale · 14
I Hear You Calling · 16
Grateful · 18
Forever You Will Stay · 19
Sister · 20
Brother · 21
Thank You God · 22
Dad · 23
Queen · 24

Neatly You	25
You Say What You Think	26
Don't Lose Sight	27
My Love	28
Being the Best	29
Pretty Girls	30
Steal	31
Do You Know Him?	32
Come to Me	33
Music	34
False Beliefs	35
Together as One	37

ACKNOWLEDGMENTS

I would like to thank God for using me to write this book. I would like to thank my husband, Otis, for all of his love, support, and encouragement. Also a big thank-you goes to all of my family and friends and everyone who has taken the time to support me. I love you all!

CHOOSE ME

I hear you calling
I hear you searching in the dark,
Anxious for light you long to see
Why do you worry?
I finished my canvas on Calvary
Trust Me
I am here
I have been waiting for you
The table is already spread
Seek Me first
Love Me
Obey Me
I choose you

Matthew 6:33

Poetry

PAIN SO DEEP

You pulled my ponytail
You chased me to the deep
Pushed me in that river
Only to feel hurt so deep
Didn't know it would shape my life
Bring feelings of skepticism and doubt
Doubt in mankind's ways
Never to be free to truly love again
Only to grow old and to look back
And to wonder, why me?
What did I do?
What did I say?
To be humiliated in this way
But in the end, only God could show me
The truth
The truth to forgive those
To love those
And to say, "Pain so deep, but not deep enough to bring defeat."
To say, "Move on, stand up, declare the way."
To say, "Rejoice: it's a brand new day!"

Matthew 5:44–48

WHO DO YOU CHOOSE?

God kept her chaste,
God kept her for His glory.
God spoke to a child,
For her to tell the story
That you're never too young to live for Him,
That you can read your Bible, spend time with Him.
You can laugh, be a kid, and be different.
It's okay to choose God
It doesn't make you weird;
Heaven and hell are for real.
Jesus said thou shalt love the Lord thy God
With all thy heart, and with all thy soul, and with all thy mind.
This is the first and great commandment,
And the second is like unto it:
Thou shalt love thy neighbor as thyself.
On these two commandments hang all the law and the prophets.
Who do you choose? What do you choose?
She chose God then;
She chooses Him now.
So can you.

Matthew 22:37–40

Poetry

YOU ARE SOMEBODY

They lied when they told you that you weren't somebody.
"You are special to Me," says God,
"And I am sorry that they hurt you."
You are dealing with pain now;
You don't understand why.
You often ask,
Why was I the victim of abuse?
Why was I mistreated by all?
Why is there never anyone there for me?
"I see you," says God.
"I see your pain;
I am healing you now
Making you strong
So that you can reach others just like you."
There are others that need you,
"But first I must heal you," says the Lord.
Don't worry about your enemies
"Vengeance is mine," says the Lord.
But some of them will come back for forgiveness;
"You must forgive even though it hurts, because
My plan is much greater, and I need you whole.
You are my child, and I shall reward and deliver you.
Trust in Me

I will be all that you need."
Just believe that you are special and that you are somebody great!

John 3:16; Romans 8:37–39

Poetry

SO TIRED, MY GOD

Up all day
He heard yelling and shouting
Can't seem to find his way
Confused, frustrated, humiliated with fear
Complaints
What is wrong?
Why the tears?
Why the sadness?
Why the madness?
Why the questions?
Why the weakness?
Just why?
But then God came in and freed that mind
Took away all the whys and
Turned that mourning into dancing
Turned that sorrow into joy
Won't He do it; Yes He will!
O Lord my God, we will give thanks unto thee forever!

Psalm 30:11–12

Poetry

THE CHILDREN TEACH YOU

God teaches you
God shows you things through your children
He makes you a better person
He teaches you patience through them
He shows you yourself
He shows you how you don't listen at times
God used the children to make you better
I am convinced of this
Because He uses mine to help me every day
May God continue to bless all the little children forever!

Matthew 19:14

FLAWED: SO WHY THE JUDGMENT?

We are all flawed
In all the same ways,
Yet we talk and decipher meanings, thinking
Our actions, lives, and meanings
Are not the same,
Only to find…that it is.
So why the judgment?
Thinking we are different,
That we don't do the same things we correct,
But yet we do.
Why the judgment?
I ask myself this question,
Only to find the true answer that God gives, which is
That every way of a man is right in his own eyes,
But the Lord pondereth the hearts.
Still thinking it's not the same…but different…
But this is why we have the judgment.

Proverbs 21:2

Poetry

LOVE IN MY HEART

Just a hug
Melts the soul.
Just a hug and smile changes the day and
Leads me to believe that I am loved
In every way.
They looked in my eyes and
Called my name and
Said I was the greatest in every way.
Children will do that, you know
Pat you on the shoulders
And tell you to keep going.
They will tilt their heads and nod and say
That we have love in our heart for you in every way.

1 Corinthians 13:13

ANGER

Didn't know you had it in you,
But it's not the real you.
It's okay now that you know what to do:
Reject it; don't accept it.
Instead, read this and declare it:
I am swift to hear, slow to speak, slow to wrath,
For the wrath of man worketh not the righteousness of God.
I will not allow anger to take control of me.
If I resist the anger, it will go.
I encourage you to
Speak God's Word and know that
If the Son therefore shall make you free, ye shall be free indeed.

John 8:36; James 1:19–20; James 4:7

Poetry

LOVE IS YOU

Courage and strength
That's you.
A mighty pillar that triumphs
That's you.
Courage and love always
In the face of many trials
An example to show us that it is Him up above
Who guides you through
Every step or fall.
Nonetheless, He leads you through them all.
I praise my God for you;
I am so blessed to have you.
Yeah, courage and strength
That's you.
A mighty pillar that triumphs
It's you!

2 Corinthians 12:9; Titus 2:7

BONDAGE

Wake up to you
Yelling, screaming,
Fighting in the hallways,
Fighting in the cells.
Slavery, abuse, and mistreatment,
Lies, deceit, and trickery
Scheming to keep me longer
Just to collect the money.
You tell me to lie and throw away the key
Just to make me weak.
They say only the strong survive,
But greater is He that is in me
Than he that is in the world.
God kept me strong;
I didn't break.
Even in the dark alone
I still didn't break.
No one ever knew
The pain, the suffering I endured…
Endured losses and loved ones,
Never able to fully
Grieve; but God knew,
And he cared enough
To never leave me.
He stood right beside me;
He even told me He was inside of me,
That He would lead and guide me
Through these trials and tribulations

Even when I couldn't see.
I understood that this was bondage
And that God intervened
And led me right behind Him.
He said, "Follow Me, Son.
Follow Me, Daughter.
I will make you fishers of men.
I will make you whole."
You have purpose;
You have strength in you;
You have a testimony.
The people need you out there,
So let's go away from this bondage;
Let's go away from this pain;
Let's go away from the misery;
And let's go together and declare the works of the Lord!

2 Corinthians 12:10; Psalm 118:6; 1 John 4:4

FAIRY TALE

You thought you knew what you wanted,
But you didn't know the price it took.
You look at all those pictures and think,
Life's like the book:
Fiction is what they like
Fiction is what they live.
Never did you imagine
Life could be so ill,
Only to realize one day
That you didn't want the fairy tale.
The fairy tale was much too complicated after all,
So why call it a fairy tale?
It was only done for show
Once you began it,
You started to say no.
This is not what I imagined
This is too hard for me.
But in the end, God
Came and corrected the dream,
Gave you a vision,
Something you could hold on to,
Because after all, the fairy tale is no longer you,
But you become the tale of what is true

A testimony that some tales can be true for those
Like me and you.

Proverbs 29:1; Proverbs 3:5–6

Poetry

I HEAR YOU CALLING

I hear your voice
Calling me,
Saying to come,
Come near Me, my child.
Hold on;
Don't forget my words.
Keep loving me
Keep loving others
Don't give up
Don't give in
I love you.
I have called you and set you apart for Myself.
You are valuable;
You are the apple of my eye.
Don't look to anything or anyone
But Me.
I am your God;
I am the beginning and the end,
For I know all things.
I have come to give you life and life more abundantly.
I have come to give you an expected end.
Draw near to Me, and I will draw near to you.
Remember I am coming quickly,
Like a thief in the night.
Hold fast your profession of faith until the end.
I am a rewarder of those who diligently seek Me.

I hear you calling, my child
Hold on.

Hebrews 10:23; 2 Peter 3:10; Hebrews 11:6; James 4:8; Zechariah 2:8; Psalm 17:8

Poetry

GRATEFUL

You are grateful, full of love
Grateful to God for His mercy, love, and faithfulness.
Your heart is full of gladness
Long days He has satisfied you with.
You are grateful
Always singing with thanksgiving,
Making melody in your heart,
Always grateful,
Truly rich and blessed with His favor, grace,
Compassion, and most of all,
God's love inside of you.
Which is why I am grateful for you!

Philippians 1:3

Poetry

FOREVER YOU WILL STAY

You're such a blessing from above;
Nothing could take away our love.
You deserve more than dresses,
More than houses,
More than rich lands.
Why? Because you're you.
You are special in every way.
A burden
I will never say.
Never were you a burden in any way.
I wrote this poem
To show you my love
And to let you know you are loved
Loved by me and by God above.
You deserve all of God's best;
I love you today,
I love you forever, Mom.
In my heart forever that's where you'll stay!

SISTER

You are beautiful as can be, with a loving heart,
Giving to those whose hearts have been broken,
Helping them to pick up the pieces.
You see,
God called you, made you beautiful and sweet.
He made you strong and complete.
You have a story and great mission to tell
To lead the lost from hell.
It's just the beginning of many great things you will do;
God will show you what to do.
I am proud to call you my sister,
Beautiful as can be with a great mission,
A journey ahead to bring the Great Commission.
I love you always, Sis.
Keep the cleaving, because you are prospering daily and believing!

BROTHER

Thank you, Brother, for being a great help.
You are always loving and kind.
Thank you, Brother, for being a great role model of mine.
God blessed you and placed you into my life,
And I am so thankful that you are a brother of mine.

Poetry

THANK YOU GOD

Lord, You are always cool,
Filled with wisdom and truth.
I love that we can talk to You anytime, day or night,
And You always provide the answers,
And they are always right.
So thank You, God,
For loving us and for always being right!

DAD

Thanks for giving me advice,
For always being there,
And for showing me that you cared.
You took time even when you were busy;
You always let me know that you were there.
I love you more than words can say;
I know that I can count on you every day.
I thank God for you, Dad, and I love you.

Poetry

QUEEN

My Queen
My beloved
My inspiration
My best friend
My help-mate
My love…
You are absolutely
Stunning and wise
I am more than smitten
I can go on forever…
I love you
I thank God
You are
My Queen.

NEATLY YOU

Fixed right in every way,
Perfectly fit, designed to stay.
Neatly you is what I say
I think you're fun, bright, and neat;
You even showed me how to be discreet.
Neatly you is what I say
You're strong, smart, and unique as a breeze;
Your smile is perfect, touching many as you lead.
Neatly you is what I say
Good taste in fashion,
Great beauty and style,
You are the woman that God designed.
God designed you perfectly; the apple of His eyes.
Neatly You is what God says!

YOU SAY WHAT YOU THINK

You say what you think
You mean what you say.
Then you think, Maybe? Should I? Should I not?
But it's okay,
Thinking everything should go your way
And that everyone should do what you say.
You judge me, then I judge back.
You get angry
Then turn your back.
I wonder why…
I just did what you showed me.
Think about others' feelings;
Think about how you would want to be treated back;
Then maybe next time you won't be so quick to react.

Matthew 7:12

Poetry

DON'T LOSE SIGHT

It's easy to lose sight,
Focus on other things than what is really in your soul to do.
Don't get distracted; just focus on what's within.
You already know the answer
Just keep focus,
Keep going,
Keep your eyes on the prize.
You already won
Just believe in it; follow it and be strong.
Trust what God has put in your soul,
And run on!

MY LOVE

My love
My king
My spouse
My best friend
Your love is better than wine
I pray for you daily
You are forever in my heart
You are my champ
You are chosen by God
Chosen for me
Special in every way
God has blessed you
And with long life will He continue to satisfy you
I love you now
Always and forever!

Song of Solomon 1:2

BEING THE BEST

Wanna be the best
Can't stand it sometimes
When others seem to be blessed
Don't wanna have this
How do you fight this?
Well, just lift your hands and recite this:
"Dear God,
Help me
Save me
Deliver me
Free me
I choose to recognize what is in me.
I will tell it to flee,
And I will depend on Thee.
Now I will move on and rejoice with Thee.
Amen.

James 4:7

Poetry

PRETTY GIRLS

You see pretty girls
It makes you mad.
You see pretty girls
Then get sad.
You see pretty girls and think, Why am I so mad?
Jealousy is as cruel as the grave;
Don't give in to it, or you will be a slave.
You should see them and be glad
You should rejoice, because we are all created in God's image,
And nothing can compare to that.
No matter what anyone told you,
You have to believe the truth:
That God made You pretty too,
And that's the end of the book.

Song of Solomon 8:6; Genesis 1:27

STEAL

Some companies will lie, cheat, steal
Aggravate you for real
But you know God knows and sees all
And justice will prevail
Watch as well as pray
Keep your eye on your accounts
And give God praise
He will bring you out!

DO YOU KNOW HIM?

"I know the man," they say,
But never serve Him, watch or pray.
It's not about what you say, but the motive is what is true.
Take a look at what's in the book:
Romans 10:9 says that if thou shalt confess with thy mouth the
Lord Jesus, and shalt believe in thine heart that God hath raised Him from
the dead, thou shalt be saved.
Romans 10:10: For with the heart man believeth unto righteousness, and
with the mouth confession is made unto salvation.
Romans 10:11: For the scripture saith, whosoever believeth on Him shall
not be ashamed.
Romans 10:12: For there is no difference between the Jew and the Greek:
for the same Lord over all is rich unto all that call upon Him.
Romans 10:13: For whosoever shall call upon the name of the Lord
Shall be saved.
Now I know Him and understand the truth
That Jesus died to save me and you.
Turn to Him today.
He is waiting, and today you can know Him and learn of Him.
John 17:3 says, And this is life eternal, that they might know thee the only
true God, and Jesus Christ, whom thou hast sent.
Romans 6:23 says that for the wages of sin is death, but the gift of God is
eternal life through Jesus Christ our Lord. Amen.

Poetry

COME TO ME

I want to live
I want to be free.
"Come to Me," Jesus said,
"I have prepared a place for you;
You shall see.
Welcome Me into your heart and soul;
Lean on Me;
I know the trials that you endured.
In this world that you are in,
Trials may come,
But trust in Me
And know that I love you, my child,
And I am with you always.
Draw nigh to Me, and I will draw nigh unto you."

1 Peter 4:1; James 4:8

Poetry

MUSIC

You tap your hands to the beat
As you sit and watch;
Then you repeat,
Not knowing that it's the music that is in your heart,
The music that is in you.
You go to that meeting and subconsciously make a beat;
You hear the drums and bass rowing;
"It's music," I say.
Music within you,
Placed there by God in every way.
Use it for His glory;
Make a joyful noise to the Lord;
Sing that melody to Him.
You are His representative.
May God bless you and be with you
As you sing His praises forever!

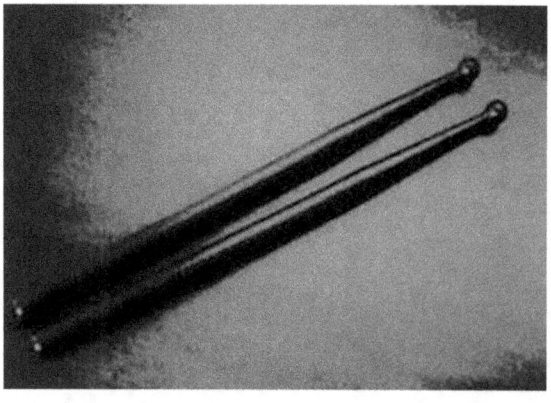

FALSE BELIEFS

She looked afraid, because they revealed what she did not have.
She looked fearful, because she thought their views would
Depict her as weak, because of what they felt she lacked.
Fearful that her reputation and beloved fans
Would now look at her differently
Although the ones that judged her after all
Were only mere mortals themselves
Judging out of jealousy,
Some out of ignorance,
Sometimes out of foolishness,
Sometimes out of just wanting to have something to say or
Out of their own insecurities or wanting to live vicariously through her.
It is a false belief when one tells you that you should have this or have that;
Our lives are not defined by what we have and what we do.
Anyone can learn and do, but what Jesus said is the only truth.
This natural life creates a depiction to some
Of what you should have accomplished
By certain time frames,
But don't get wrapped into it
Don't measure your success by what someone else did.
What they desire is what they desire;
What you desire is what you desire.
Just know why you want something:
Let God be your role model;
Let Jesus be your guide.
Maybe it was not your time to have what you thought you needed
Or your time to do what others learned to do.
Your looks and age do not matter;

In the Bible age never mattered to God.
Some just began their lives
In their forties, fifties,
Sixties, and beyond.
Don't let the false belief get you down.
Instead, believe that you are strong in the Lord
And in the power of His might.
Just let Jesus be your guide.

Ephesians 6:10; Jeremiah 29:11

TOGETHER AS ONE

Fathers and mothers
Sisters and brothers
All family members
All mankind
Everything that has breath
Let us rejoice
Let us come together to worship and sing
Let us come together to praise our God
Who is greatly to be praised
Let us love
Let us crucify the flesh daily
Let us comfort and help one another
We are strong together
Let us walk in unity on one accord, lifting up the Name of Jesus
Let us praise Him, for it is He who has given us breath and life
Let us rejoice and sing praises to Him forever and ever!

Psalm 150:6

POETRY

JUST A WALK
WITH GOD

www.ingramcontent.com/pod-product-compliance
Lightning Source LLC
Chambersburg PA
CBHW070404240426
43661CB00056B/2534